D1294073

VLAMINCK

Vlaminck

BY JEAN SELZ

CROWN PUBLISHERS, INC. ▴ NEW YORK

Title page: ANDRÉ DERAIN
Portrait of Vlaminck. 1903
(16" × 14 ½")
Private Collection, Paris

Translated from the French by:

GRAHAM SNELL

SAILING BOATS AT CHATOU. 1906. (15" × 18") Capt. Molyneux Collection, Paris

Maurice de Vlaminck was a big man. I am not referring to his broad chest and thirteenstone bulk, but to his exuberant personality and to everything in his life that represented movement, noise, sudden fierce desire, laughter, temper, revolt and violence – all of which seem to accord so well with the way he painted that one might be tempted to try to explain his art purely in terms of his life.

But with an artist things are never so simple. So let us forget, for a moment, that Vlaminck was a racing cyclist in 1893, at the age of 17, a double-bass player in his regimental band in 1897, an anarchist and editor of the journal *Le Libertaire* in 1899, a violinist in 1900 (he specialised in slow waltzes and boisterous czardas, which he played in the "gypsy" orchestras of the *Petit Casino de Montmartre* and the *Café des Princes*), a weight lifter, a billiards player,

Three Figures (the title according to Vlaminck: " The Brothel ")
Woodcut (8½" × 7"). Dr. Sigmond Pollag Collection, Zurich

and in turn an enthusiastic sculler, Graeco-Roman wrestler, motor cyclist, car driver and, throughout his life, a lover of good living. Let us just consider the remarkable energy that these predominantly physical activities implied and, while not for a moment forgetting the important rôle that the more or less controlled unleashing of his vitality played in his work as a painter, let us look at his painting and try to determine to what extent it accords with, or is in opposition to, the great movements that have torn like a hurricane through the world of the arts ever since the turn of the century.

Vlaminck's habit of not dating his canvases makes it impossible to determine the exact chronological order of his work. Certain of his biographers and even some galleries have tried to give a date to his paintings, and the fact that they are often so wide of the mark does not make things easier for those who are concerned with historical truth. But although we cannot follow the painter's development from year to year with complete certainty, we can at least plot the various stages that divide his work into distinctive periods.

The first, dating from his early years when he was still casting about uncertainly for a style, lasted from 1900 to 1903. The Fauve period began in 1904 and went on till 1907. Then came the Cézanne period, more difficult to circumscribe, for though it was very much in evidence in 1907 and remained a dominating factor until 1910, nevertheless a number of pictures he painted in later years revealed, from time to time, a nostalgia for these years which for many painters opened up new vistas, and were to change the destiny of art. Thus it was about 1911 that a new and important period began for Vlaminck, one in which his personality took shape, free of all influence, and this stage in his career lasted approximately until 1927. Then followed the last period, and a long one, which in spite of occasional fluctuations, was to preserve its character unchanged till he died in 1958. In the preceding years there had been signs – in particular the general tone of his colours – of what was to be this final stage in his career; but it is a period which is still distinctly recognisable, above all by a marked lyricism whose inspiration we shall examine later.

The interest of these important divisions, in whose framework we shall explore the painter's work, lies not so much in the fact that they help us to trace his development – and I should not like to give the impression that they are more exact than they really are – but they are interesting above all because they help us understand how in his painting Vlaminck sometimes fought against himself; and they also enable us to see through apparent contradictions to the constant essence of his artistic spirit.

THE SEEDS OF VIOLENCE

A man smoking a pipe, wearing a red hat, with a red silk handkerchief round his neck, dressed in brown, and painted without a thought for form or composition, in wide streaks of colour scored across the canvas (recalling the crudely sculptured marionettes in the wood that were once to be seen in Flemish towns) – such is *le Père Bouju* which Vlaminck painted in 1900.

It was certainly not a carefully executed painting; indeed it was done with impetuous zest. But the force in the expression (even though it almost became a caricature) and the freedom in execution – these and his energy, his disregard of all narrow principles, pointed clearly, on one hand, to what throughout the whole of Vlaminck's life was to constitute the violent character of his art, and on the other, to a kind of painting that a few years later was to be called Expressionism.

Where, then, had Vlaminck learnt to paint? He was twenty-four and was living in Chatou, where he shared a miserable studio with a certain Derain, the son of a dairyman, who was also resolved, in spite of family opposition, to be a painter. (They had met that same year on a train.) Vlaminck had learnt the rudiments of painting some ten years before from a member of the *Société des Artistes Français* called Robichon, an anecdotal painter, and from a harness-maker from Vésinet who in his spare time poured his naïve enthusiasm into painting portraits on pieces of glass. It is enough to look at Vlaminck's earliest pictures, far removed in their revolutionary fervour from all academic influence but at the same time not at all unsophisticated, to realise how far behind he had left his "teachers" and that if he was an apprentice he was also his own master. However, it is possible that the bright glossy colours favoured by the Vésinet harness-maker had influenced the young painter to a certain extent. The same can be said of the three statuettes from Dahomey and the Ivory Coast, unearthed in a *bistrot* in Argenteuil in 1905; they opened his eyes to Negro art, of which he was to become a very keen collector.

If we are still struck by the originality of *le Père Bouju*, even today when contemporary art has taught us not to be surprised at anything, how astounding it must have seemed in the period when Vlaminck was beginning to paint! Little wonder, then, that the public knew only a small part of the work done by the great artists of the day. What they knew, and what held pride of place in the *Salons* and won the praise and support of official bodies, was the academic, anecdotal (pseudo-realist) or historical painting taught at the *Ecole des Beaux-Arts*. Good painting – and the expression is too weak to describe some of the masterpieces of this period – remained more often than not on the fringe – or in other words, outside the big exhibitions. But the question remains: where were the painters who had overcome the critics' hostility and had achieved a certain notoriety? Where, indeed, was the *avant-garde*?

In 1900, Picasso – who was not yet launched on his "blue period" – arrived in Paris while Gauguin was landing in Tahiti for the second time. Cézanne was working on his *Grandes Baigneuses*; he had already painted most of his best pictures and was nearing the end of his life. As an expression of his admiration for him, Maurice Denis painted the large picture that can be seen today in the *Musée d'Art Moderne* in Paris, which is entitled *Homage to Cézanne*. Monet was painting his *Nympheas*, Renoir his *Landscape with Nude* and Pissarro his *Self-Portrait*. Sisley had been dead a year. And, in fact, Impressionism had been on the decline for at least fifteen years. Neo-Impressionism, which had succeeded it around 1886, with Seurat, Signac, Cross and a number of others, had itself been fading away ever since the death in 1891 of Seurat, its chief protagonist. Signac, the youngest of the group and the

INTERIOR. 1903-4. (25½" × 21") Musée National d'Art Moderne, Paris

The Banks of the Seine at Carrières-sur-Seine. 1906
(21" × 25½") Stéphane Faniel Collection, Paris

10

MARLY-LE ROI. 1906
(32" × 23") Kaganovitch Collection, Paris

LE PÈRE BOUJU. 1900   DANCER FROM THE "RAT MORT". 1906
(29" × 19") Madame Maurice de Vlaminck Collection   (28½" × 25") A. Fries Collection, Paris
Rueil-la-Gadelière

Woman's Head. 1906. Woodcut (12½" × 11½"). Dr. Sigmond Pollag Collection, Zurich

14

Woman's Head. 1910. Woodcut (13" × 10")
Dr.Sigmond Pollag Collection, Zurich

most ardent adherent of its theories, was to stick to the " dot technique " in his painting, but nevertheless the need for a form of expression that was free of all scientific theory was already making itself felt.

However, the Neo-Impressionist influence had left a temporary but significant mark on the work of Van Gogh, and we must bear this in mind when we come to examine the way Vlaminck developed.

And so the great movements that had revolutionised painting at the end of the nineteenth century had run their course and there seemed to be nothing else destined to succeed them. The young painters of the *avant-garde* of 1900 were making little more than

SAINT-CLOUD. 1910. (13" × 16") Dr. Sigmond Pollag Collection, Zurich

Bougival. 1905
$(31\frac{1}{2}" \times 39")$ Emery Reves Collection

WOMAN IN A STRAW HAT. 1906. (32" × 25½") Private Collection, Paris

PORTRAIT OF DERAIN. 1905. (10½" × 8½") Private Collection, Paris

FLOWERS. 1909. Kahnweiler Collection, Paris

piecemeal experiments, standing as they were at the cross-roads of conflicting tendencies. The pictures that one can say belong to the years when Vlaminck was at the beginning of his career – 1903-1904 – were not all painted in the vigorous style of *Père Bouju*. Certain landscapes, such as *The Garden* and *Quai Sganzin à Bougival*, which are more solid and carefully composed, are painted in cooler colours. This restraint, which expressed itself in colours that were neither very bright nor very sombre, would seem to indicate that while still groping uncertainly for his true personality, Vlaminck tried temporarily to tame his fiery temperament. But in doing this he was only struggling against the very essence of his creative force. He was soon to realise this and *Interior*, one of the most curious and significant pictures of the latter part of this period, seems to represent a synthesis of the painter's conflicting tendencies; attracted as he was by hot bright colours, he was also aware of the dramatic aspect of things, and this gave him a preference for darker tones. In this picture, painted in fairly cool colours, the clash of red (the ground and the window) and green (the woman and the table) seems to stem from a compelling need to react against the general sombre tonality. Looking at this *Interior*, one might say that here Fauvism was beginning to burgeon from the depths of the painter's subconscious, and that is why this picture is so important to an understanding of his later work.

It was in 1901 that an important event occurred in Vlaminck's life, and one that three years later was to have a decisive influence on his work. This was the occasion when he first saw an exhibition of Van Gogh's paintings, at the Bernheim-Jeune Gallery. "I came away from that exhibition," he wrote in *Portraits avant Décès*, " profoundly moved".

Could it be that it was because Vlaminck was first and foremost a Fleming that he had a particularly sensitive understanding of Van Gogh's painting? In any case it is interesting to note that the extraordinarily dramatic transformation of landscape that Van Gogh produced by means of luminous colour – that apparent contradiction between what we are in the habit of calling " joyful colours " and the brooding tragedy that they acquired for the purpose of defying or veiling – it was this that was to be one of the most striking features of Vlaminck's painting.

Now, if the dramatisation of landscape by using sombre colours was to mark, some time later, a new phase in Vlaminck's work, we cannot help noticing that this was to come about, curiously enough, at a time in his life when he was more at peace with himself and was enjoying greater security. On the other hand, the beginning of the " joyful colour " period coincided with the years of his youth, years of extremely depressing difficulties when he was living in story-book poverty with the woman he had married in 1894, when he was eighteen, and the two daughters of their marriage. Vlaminck, who wrote novels and memoirs, has more than once described these pathetic years when he sometimes went twenty-four hours without eating, and lived in nightmare conditions in the squalid house on the Nanterre plain, with the most desolate countryside all around, and when the only money he made was from the violin lessons he gave in the evenings. "If," he wrote, "there is sometimes a sense of brooding tragedy in my painting, I don't think it begins to suggest the dreariness of that place."

The image of this sad Vlaminck is hidden sometimes under that of the gay companion described by Francis Carco. "Vlaminck, the disreputable-looking habitué of suburban inns, pipe in mouth, with his bicycle, his polo-neck jersey..." And Guillaume Apollinaire was right when he wrote: "Maurice de Vlaminck has a Flemish sense of the joy of life. His painting is a *kermis*. He laughs with his whole being." We find these two aspects of the painter's character reflected in his work, but the mood of any particular picture did not by any means always echo the conditions in which he was living when he painted it. And this suggests that for Vlaminck, as for Van Gogh, painting was to a certain extent the act by which he rebelled against fate. It was to escape his destiny, to

STILL-LIFE – FRUITS. 1908. (28½" × 36") Emil G. Buehrle Collection, Zurich

STILL-LIFE – APPLES. 1906. ($21\frac{1}{2}$" × 18") Private Collection, Paris

defy or shut out its harsh contrasts, that he gave himself up to the delirious joys of colour. He could have said what Seurat said: "Let's go and intoxicate ourselves with light once again. It's consoling."

A FAUVE AMONG FAUVES

One could never imagine Rembrandt playing the big drum. But Vlaminck, yes – one can well imagine him doing so. And during his military service he often did: putting aside his double-bass, he played the big drum with great zest on regimental marches. Neither is it surprising that he should have added to his range of colours those of the various instruments. He wrote in *Paysages et Personnages*, one of his books of memoirs: "In the band that I conducted I had decided to use only brass instruments, cymbals and the big drum, which for me were just tubes of colour".

And this was the coruscating music of the Fauves, which so scandalised the public and the critics, who were accustomed to a more subdued kind of painting. By bringing about a revolution in the use of colour, these painters not only scandalised the bourgeoisie, they caused them great anxiety. Vlaminck himself wrote: "The bourgeoisie thought they could buy up the arts just as they bought up silk, cotton and steel." From the moment painters dared to paint trees red, landscape lost its attraction for such people. "As," he wrote, "I did not have to obey any rules and did not care a hang for what people thought of me, I gave my revolutionary instincts a free rein and my only preconceived idea was to please myself and, in that excellent phrase of my father's, 'waste my time'."

Argenteuil. 1909. Woodcut (7" × 9½"). Dr. Sigmond Pollag Collection, Zurich

HOUSEBOATS. 1906
(19½" × 28½") Private Collection, Paris

SOUTHAMPTON. 1911
(24" × 19½") Private Collection, Pully, Switzerland

THE BARGE. 1905-6
(23½" × 28½") Ishibashi Collection, Tokio

BASKET OF GRAPES. 1920
Private Collection, New York

SELF-PORTRAIT. 1912
◁ (18" × 21½")
Private Collection

THE RAILWAY BRIDGE AT CHATOU. 1908. $(23\frac{1}{2}'' \times 28\frac{1}{2}'')$
Private Collection, New York

TOWER BRIDGE. 1911
Private Collection, New York

THE OLD PORT AT MARSEILLES. 1913
(36" × 28½") Private Collection, New York

32

Although the name " Fauves ", which of course was pejorative, was coined in 1905, the year when Matisse, Derain, Vlaminck, Manguin, Friesz, Puy and Valtat, who all painted with more or less hot, bright colours, exhibited at the *Salon d'Automne*, this kind of painting had made its appearance a year before in a number of pictures, but principally those of Vlaminck. In fact, Fauvism dates from 1904 and its pure bright flame only really shone for three years. But long before, Van Gogh had blazed the trail for Fauvism with his new conception of the play of light and his technique of alternating splashes of colour.

The colours that Gauguin used in some of his landscapes – *Windmill in Brittany*, *The Ford* (Leningrad Museum) – have sometimes led to his being called a forerunner of Fauvism. But his technique and approach were far removed from those of Fauvism. In any case, he never influenced Vlaminck, who described his painting as " devoid of natural feeling "

THE WAY INTO THE VILLAGE (THE FRANCHEVILLE ROAD). 1922. Lithograph (9" × 13")
Dr. Sigmond Pollag Collection, Zurich

The Old Port at Marseilles. 1913. Woodcut (10" × 13"). Dr. Sigmond Pollag Collection, Zurich

and wrote that it had never moved him. Van Gogh, on the other hand, he recognised as the source of at least part of his inspiration, and he was to be influenced by him for several years.

When one looks at a painting like *Gauguin's Armchair*, which Van Gogh painted in Arles in 1888, one is reminded of what he wrote one day: "I have tried to express with red and green the terrible human passions". Perhaps this stemmed from a need to justify his bold methods to himself, for there is no " terrible passion " in this empty chair, the back of whose straw seat is occupied only by a candlestick and two books. Yet the brilliant splashes of red and green are placed beside a mauve shadow – exactly like the pictures of the first Fauves or of those who were soon to join their group, which was called, rather abusively, the Chatou School. Van Dongen's *Reclining Nude*, Braque's *Countryside at Collioure* and Dufy's *The Three Sunshades* – the inspiration behind the fierce colours of all these was still Van Gogh's. But it was not only with his choice and arrangement of colours that Van Gogh made such an impression on Vlaminck and fired his admiration to the point where he said, " I love

Van Gogh more than my father ". What also filled him with wonder was the extraordinary animation that his alternating splashes of colour lent to his landscapes. In the pictures Van Gogh painted in his last years, which he spent in Paris, Arles, Saint-Rémy and Auvers-sur-Oise, the skies, trees, houses, wheatfields and even faces are shaded in with great heavy lines and brought to life by those dancing curves, like little tongues of flame, which testify to the feverish speed at which he painted.

One can see in the way Van Gogh threw himself into his work, the fear that he would not have time to paint all that he dreamed of painting, just as if he had had a premonition of his early death. But this tremendous tempo of work accorded with his final conception of what painting is. In a letter to his brother Théo, he wrote one day: " I'm beginning to realise that some of the landscapes I painted faster than ever before, are the best I have done." The great interest he took in Daumier's paintings and above all in those of Monticelli, can

Sails. 1913. Woodcut (11" × 14"). Dr. Sigmond Pollag Collection, Zurich

STILL-LIFE – CUBIST FORMS. 1910
Private Collection, New York

37

STILL-LIFE. 1917
Private Collection, New York

◁ VASE OF FLOWERS. 1916
Chester Dale Collection, New York

STILL-LIFE. 1917
Lewisohn Collection, New York

40

be partly explained by the fact that, as he actually wrote, he saw them as pictures painted " with great speed ". We know that this way of working is very much in favour today with the painters who come under the heading of "abstract action painters". The term " action painting " was not in use then, but basically it will serve as a definition of Van Gogh's technique. And Van Gogh was to bequeath it to Vlaminck, who said one day: " I work very fast, just as I eat."

On the other hand, while the Fauves were showing their work to the public at the *Salon d'Automne* of 1905, an exhibition of Van Gogh's work was being held in Dresden where, in that same year, the *Brücke* was founded. Fauvism was soon to make its headquarters there with, among others, Van Dongen and Ernst-Ludwig Kirchner, whose work was to bear its imprints for a long time. But by far the most important offshoot of the *Brücke* was Expressionism, a movement that was only to be granted tardy recognition in France. Now, if we have always regarded the motive force of this movement as basically Nordic, we

Bowl of Fruit. 1920. Lithograph ($18\frac{1}{2}$" × 25"). Dr. Sigmond Pollag Collection, Zurich

Montparnasse Crossroads. 1918. Indian ink (15" × 18"). Dr. Sigmond Pollag Collection, Zurich

must not forget to add to the names of Edvard Munch, James Ensor and Emil Nolde, that of Van Gogh who, here again, reveals himself as a forerunner.

Thus it seems quite natural that in spite of the differences that were to separate Expressionism from Fauvism, both of which stemmed from Van Gogh, we should find them both present, separately or merged, in the work of Vlaminck.

We know that the most obvious characteristic of Fauve painting is the use of pure colours. All the painters in the group made abundant use of them, and it was for this that they were most severely criticised. " A paint-pot has been thrown at the public," wrote Camille Mauclair. But the famous expression, "tube against canvas", which Vlaminck himself used, should not be taken too literally. Certainly, pure red was the Fauves' favourite colour, and doubtless one can say – particularly if one finds it amusing to think of the bright blushes the word " Fauve " can produce – that they "saw red". But if we look at their most glowing pictures from close up, we realise that along with the pure colours there are plenty that are not pure.

An example is Vlaminck's *The Red Trees*, in which a landscape of fields and houses is seen from a foreground of tree-trunks; these trunks are painted in about ten more or less subtle shades and the brown, the blue, the pink and the orange are juxtaposed with a whole range of reds. If, however, the colours in this picture seem to be of a striking intensity, it is first and foremost because of this very juxtaposition which shuts out all shadow and three-dimensional effect; it is also because each form is outlined in Prussian blue. This technique, which Vlaminck often employed during this period (two examples – and there are others – are *A Street in Marly-le-Roi* and *The Hills around Rueil*), made it possible to slip a blue in among the glowing colours, with which its coldness contrasted. And the contrast

Saint-Leu-Taverny. 1919. Lithograph (15" × 18½"). Dr. Sigmond Pollag Collection, Zurich

clearly made the picture " sing " and remedied the blurred effect which the absence of shadow tended to produce. But in certain cases – *The Hills around Rueil* in particular – when perspective has not been observed, the background of the landscape comes surging forward. In a number of other pictures – *The Red Trees*, for instance – the blue outlines in the distance are paler, thus giving a better idea of space.

All this means that the pure tone and other Fauve techniques were not systematically applied by Vlaminck – any more than they were by his fellow Fauves. The fanfare could sometimes be muted. In some of their pictures, Matisse, Marquet, Friesz and Van Dongen made use of colours that were obviously toned down, and in landscapes that were predominantly warm and vivid they were thus able to achieve variety. And that is why we find a much greater similarity between a Vlaminck picture and one by Derain than between two of Vlaminck's. The Fauves also adopted the Pointillist technique. Derain was to use it for a time, during his stay in London in 1905; and Vlaminck sometimes

Houses in Martigues. Woodcut (10" × 13")

THE OISE VALLEY. 1917
Perls Galleries, New York

45

THE CHURCH AT AUVERS-SUR-OISE (Homage to Van Gogh). 1925. (25½" × 19½")
Henri Gaffié Collection, Beaulieu-sur-mer

"DEAR FRIEND" (M. Itasse). 1924. (25½" × 19½") Dr. A. Roudinesco Collection, Paris

THE ROAD. 1926
Private Collection, New York

48

came very near to it with the small rectangular patches of colour which brought his pictures to dancing life.

But in terms of technique, Vlaminck's Fauve pictures can be divided into two main groups: those in which there is clear evidence of Van Gogh's influence, and those which belong to what one might call pure Fauvism. These pictures do not represent two successive phases of the painter's work; for if the first style made its appearance in 1904, we nevertheless recognise its characteristic features in the pictures he painted in 1907. Doubtless Vlaminck was equally fond of the two styles, and he was constantly alternating them. Sometimes they were brought into play on one and the same canvas, as is shown by *Couple in the Country*, a perfect example of a synthesis of these two styles whose differences did not prevent them from blending. The two figures, partly dressed in blue, are seated in the centre of the picture at the foot of a red tree; the man has an orange moustache, and the woman's hair is of the same colour; both these figures are painted in wide brush-strokes and sketched in with a blue line. This is pure Fauvism. But the surrounding area – grass, flowers (or bushes? it is impossible to tell) – is treated in a quite different manner: a great whirl of colour, painted in long streaks of green, red, yellow and orange, seems to encircle the couple like a mass of flame. In these darting brush-strokes and in the circular movement with which they set the landscape whirling like some fantastic roundabout, we recognise Van Gogh's influence.

And this influence was to be even more striking and far-reaching in *The Chestnut-Grove at Jonchère*. Here is one of the first instances, perhaps the first, when Vlaminck seems to have come under the spell of a lyricism which he was to abandon, a little later but for just a few years, only to give himself up to it again, and this time for the rest of his life. But by then he had embraced a quite different technique, and today we should be more likely to find echoes of the particular lyricism of *The Chestnut-Grove* in some of Pignon's recent pictures.

In some of Vlaminck's other landscapes one is aware of the part that Van Gogh had played in shaping his vision. But conscious, no doubt, of this influence, he allowed it to obtrude only in his nudes and female figures (sometimes it was combined with small rectangular patches of colour, contrasting in their brevity with the generally long brush-strokes of Van Gogh), almost as if he wanted to avoid Van Gogh's style when treating subjects that Van Gogh had also treated. Belonging to this series of pictures are *Nude with Black Stockings*, *Nude on a Divan*, *Woman with a Hat* (standing), painted in 1905, *Woman with a Hat* (seated), painted in 1906, and *Dancer from the "Rat Mort"*, in which, perhaps because of the cooler, more sober tonality of the colours, the painter had achieved a compelling power of expression.

These pictures, whose minute daubs of colour make a more or less gaudy patchwork, all seem to have conserved, precisely because of the technique with which they were painted, something of the pictorial spirit that, with the advent of pure Fauvism, was to go somewhat out of fashion. On the other hand, they represent a true liberation from artificial

THE GREEN TREE. 1924. Lithograph (9" × 11½") Dr. Sigmond Pollag Collection, Zurich

systems of painting, and are the third act in the historic revolution in the treatment of colour, of which the first two were Impressionism and Neo-Impressionism.

It is here that Vlaminck found his happiest mode of expression, when his fiery rebellious spirit was sublimated by landscape so that in spite of an obvious intoxication with colour, he was able to maintain a perfect balance between a realistic conception of the structure of what he saw, and the dazzling vision of what he imagined. André Lhote's curious remark, " One only sees well when one is dazzled ", here takes on its full meaning.

Pictures such as *The Houseboat, Bougival,* and *A Street in Marly-le-Roi,* which are typical examples of pure Fauvism, enable us to list their main characteristics. The outline drawing, done in a broken line of dark blue, is very obvious; there is an unnatural predominance of warm colours, in particular of vermilion (frequently juxtaposed with green);

50

there are wide sweeps of colour laid on in only moderately thick layers; and lastly, the problem of volume is solved by eschewing three-dimensional form and, more often than not, shadow.

The sense of gaiety, of sunny festivity, which comes up with such force from these paintings in which Nature, all decked out, gives the impression that everything is burning in the summer furnace, that everything is crying out with the joy of being alive and of giving itself up uninhibitedly to the light of a low-slung sun – this is in sharp contrast to the Flemish conception of landscape where great attention is paid to aerial perspective, to the " side-play " of *clair-obscur* and to what Corot called " the soul's inner light ", and where the person looking at the picture is made to enter into an intimate relationship with its various constituent elements. The way that the Fauves flooded their picture with light seems to point to the

THE BRIDGE OVER THE OISE AT MÉRY. 1925. Lithograph (9½" × 13½")
Dr. Sigmond Pollag Collection, Zurich

lesson, which has a singularly modern ring, that Diderot taught: " Light up your subjects with your own sun, which will not be that of Nature."

The freeing of colour from all subjection to volume thus represented a step forward in the sense that colour became a subjective consideration; and some years later, painters were to remember this and profit by it. From dispensing with volume it was only one step further to dispensing with the object itself, and if this step was taken boldly by others, one cannot forget that without realising it, Vlaminck helped on this movement towards an ever greater and more imperious freedom of expression.

But could Vlaminck go any further along this road that led to a new revolution in painting? And could he keep within the limits of Fauvism and still avoid shutting himself up in the conventions of a system? In fact, he never fell into the error of seeing painting in exclusively Fauve terms. Thus he could not commit himself to a path that he could not see, and one that he would have turned away from, had he been able to see it. But when one remembers

The Bridge at Chatou. 1913. Woodcut (10" × 14½"). Dr. Sigmond Pollag Collection, Zurich

VALMONDOIS. 1925. Gouache. Dr. A. Roudinesco Collection, Paris

how short-lived Fauvism was, it seems unlikely that he ever exhausted all its possibilities. It is enough, for example, to look at a number of exceptional pictures, such as *Portrait of Derain*, which Vlaminck painted in 1905, to realise how regrettable it is that he left us so few portraits of this type. His still-lifes are equally few and far between. And *The Barge*, one of the most dazzling landscapes he did in 1906, has such a radiant harmony of tones, with its light blues, its yellows and its orange, that we are prompted to think that in the realm of typical Fauve subjects, Vlaminck had not said all that he could have said.

But in 1906 Vlaminck was thirty. The young paint-splasher's spirit of revolt had accorded so well with his fiery, impetuous style of painting; but now the rôle of rebel and the more

Lithograph for an illustration to Raymond Radiguet's book " Le Diable au corps"

cautious, if not wiser, man that he had become, went in uneasy harness. In that year an event took place which naturally counted for a lot in the life of an artist who was still facing an uncertain future, and it was to bring him both decisive encouragement and a lessening of his difficulties: Ambroise Vollard, one of the most far-seeing art dealers of the day, bought up all his pictures, for the sum – large for those days – of six thousand francs. At last Vlaminck had the satisfaction of seeing his painting taken seriously and of being

54

Lithograph for an illustration to Georges Duhamel's book, "Les Hommes abandonnés"

REFLECTIONS. 1925. Private Collection, New York

assured, for a time at least, of the security without which he was hampered in the pursuit of his art.

It was not long after this that he began to re-examine the question of his method of painting, and new problems of technique and composition led him to a radical revision of his ideas. But until the following year he remained faithful to the Fauve style, which is still very pure in *The Country Lunch* and *The Big Tree*, and to Van Gogh's influence which is very much in evidence in the alternating splashes of colour in *The Road*. But in a number of other pictures dating from this period, the colours are already subdued – significantly enough. The flames of Fauvism were nearly spent. A new Vlaminck was about to be born.

56

UNDER THE AEGIS OF THE " SAD FRIEND "

Few events have had such a direct influence on the history of painting, and produced so many repercussions, as the retrospective exhibition of Cézanne's work at the *Salon d'Automne* of 1907, the year following the painter's death. That so many painters, and two such different painters as Picasso and Vlaminck, should experience, in the presence of a style of painting that was totally opposed to their own, a shock that was to change their whole approach – here was the first sign of the tremendous upheaval of which Cézanne was the harbinger.

One can say that for most of the painters that drew inspiration for new forms of expression from Cézanne's work, and particularly for Vlaminck, Derain and Braque, Cézanne represented a victory of form over colour. Obsessed with what had been discovered about the connection beween colour and light, the Impressionists and Neo-Impressionists had neglected the problem of form; and those for whom drawing had become an integral part of their

Bridge on the River Eure at Pacy. Woodcut ($6\frac{1}{2}$" $\times$ 9")

The River Oise at Sergy. 1924. Etching (9" × 12½"). Dr. Sigmond Pollag Collection, Zurich

questings – Manet, Degas, Van Gogh, Toulouse-Lautrec, Gauguin and Picasso (who had come to the end of his " pink period ") – still thought of drawing in largely traditional terms. Cézanne had for the first time challenged these traditional ideas, not by turning his back on discipline but by imposing on himself a new discipline which had led to a revival of interest in the plastic aspect of form.

It was when Vlaminck was in full Fauve flight that, surprisingly enough, he suddenly changed course and followed in the footsteps of the man he was one day to call " the sad friend ". But even more curious is the fact that while the pictures in which Cézanne's influence was strongly present show us something of the pessimistic side of his nature, they should nevertheless express a conception of landscape that is much more dramatic than Cézanne's.

From the year 1907 this change went on taking place in Vlaminck's work; at first, perhaps, it was fairly slow – slow, at least, if we are to consider the landscape entitled *Chatou* as one of the first pictures in which this new tendency is apparent, and in which the " style bâtonnets " is prevalent in the alternating touches of colour. In *Bathers*, an unusual subject for Vlaminck, we find an echo of Cézanne's *Bathers*, whose influence was to become apparent again in 1912 in the *Bathers* of Kirchner who went against the march of events by turning to Fauvism some fifteen years later. Left without its early zealots, except for Matisse who, in his own way, was to persist with certain of its characteristic features in his later work, Fauvism was thus, at intervals, to go on influencing a small number of painters. It survived, we notice, in some of the pictures of Mondrian (*Windmill in the Sun c. 1911*), Jawlensky (*Self-Portrait*, 1912), Miro (*The Path at Ciurana*, 1917) and a number of other painters.

It was above all between 1908 and 1910 that Vlaminck was dominated by Cézanne's influence. Doubtless he found that in applying these principles of construction, which married, within the general architecture of composition, a feeling for colour which was more subtle than that of the Fauves, to a more explicitly rendered energy of form, he discovered a new and greater force of expression. The sloping planes, the contrasts of light and shade, the introduction of darker shades into the overall tonality of a picture – these enabled him to indulge his taste for violence through mastery of form where once he had done it through glowing colour.

The Farm at Bretoncelles. 1925. Etching (7" × 10½"). Dr. Sigmond Pollag Collection, Zurich

Portrait of a Woman
1924
Lithograph
(9" × 6")
Dr. Sigmond Pollag
Collection
Zurich

Nesles-la-Vallée The River Sausseron. Lithograph (7¹/₂″ × 9¹/₂″). Dr. Sigmond Pollag, Zurich

It was now that Vlaminck experimented with new colours and discovered a dramatic aspect of landscape – discovered it but did not then express it – which eventually led to his lyricism. If the word " pessimism " comes to mind when one looks at these pictures from which all Fauve joy has disappeared, the reason lies no doubt in this very disappearance. But perhaps we should be nearer the truth if we saw in it an agonising need to protest, with an element of blind anger, against what he regarded as the curses of our artificial civilisation. " I am surprised," he said (in an essay entitled *This is my Testament* which he wrote in 1956) " that I have been able to resist up to now the scientific barbarity of the civilised human species."

This fierce plunge into Nature – which for him, a landscape painter, was not merely a source of subjects to paint but meant so much to him that he was eventually to go and live permanently in the country – saved him from all the inventions and features of modern life by which, as a lover of rustic simplicity, he felt he was menaced. But as with all great loves where there is an element of torment and sometimes a giving of oneself that seems to verge on madness, Vlaminck's great love for Nature could not fail gradually to develop into an overriding passion, and this lent a growing dramatic tension to his art. The combination of uneasy asceticism and surging tenderness to be found in the landscapes he painted in this period, gives them a charm and poetic quality that are unique in his work. Particularly good examples are *St. Denis Race-course*, *A House Reflected in Water*, *Puteaux* and *Bois de la Jonchère*; in these pictures each component part has, in its poise, the charm of a hesitation and seems to suggest rather than assert that it belongs to the colour covering it. There is a similar delicacy of vision in some of the still-lifes and in a *Self-Portrait*, one of Vlaminck's masterpieces dating from 1910, in which there is a hint of humour in the pipe and the bowler hat.

The painters who had adopted Cézanne's geometrical principles of form, were, as we know, to move towards an increasingly extreme interpretation of them, and this was the way that led, logically enough, to Cubism. Nearly all the painters who, sooner or later and to

Spring. 1925. Lithograph (10" × 14"). Dr. Sigmond Pollag Collection, Zurich

varying degrees, accepted the Cubist discipline – Braque, Picasso, Léger, Hayden, Lhote, Marcoussis – went through this phase which was often only a prelude to pure Cubist paintings, but which nevertheless produced some very remarkable work.

But what of Vlaminck? How far was he going to follow Cézanne? Pictures such as *Still-life – Pitcher*, *Factory Chimney at Puteaux*, *Still-life* and *Cubist Forms*, show that the moment was very near when he would no longer need an outside source of inspiration as he had himself already broken away from traditional perspective. With this advent of a new geometry which embraced both colour and volume, houses, trees, tables and fruit-dishes seemed to be on the verge of the final disintegration that preceded complete surrender to Cubism.

Yet neither Vlaminck nor Derain ever rallied to the Cubist banner. Derain turned to a form of expression whose inspiration was Classical. As for Vlaminck, the profound repugnance that he felt for Cubism was to develop into nothing less than hatred. He saw it as a blight that had descended on painting. "Cubism," he wrote in later years, "was the negation of the art of painting. For years it wrought dreadful havoc." And, in his *Conversations avec Marcel Sauvage*: "Painters have torn the flesh from painting. They have dehumanised it, killed it. And now they have shut away the body. They have put it in the Cubist coffin."

It is obvious that even though he helped Cézanne's theories into favour by his own important contribution to their development, Vlaminck had never for a moment imagined where they would lead to. The Cubist theories were a formulation of an intellectualised vision of art, and they were always deeply alien to him. They ran counter to his nature and his tastes, and to the enticements of a realism which attached little value to theory but which appealed to him through his literary sense of humour, to which the one or two novels he wrote bear witness.

Perhaps he felt a kind of disappointment at finding that all he had accomplished in his Cézanne period – and it includes some of his very finest work – now merely came into the category of "Pre-Cubism". The success of Cubism, which was tardy but eventually ensured its recognition as one of the great movements in modern painting, was in fact to push into the background what had led up to it. In any case, Vlaminck was to follow a quite different path; he shook off Cézanne's influence but preserved a certain severity in his new way of depicting Nature.

There had already been an indication of this new approach at the end of his Cézanne period and even (if we can take 1908, the date attributed to *Railway-bridge at Chatou*, as correct) at the high noon of this period. Be that as it may, this picture seems to be one of the first in which Vlaminck, turning away from the technique of broken-up planes, was looking both for a more Classical type of construction and a freer use of colour. At the same time, along with the predominantly green tonality of his pictures, there was also a touch of brutality in the abundant use he made of black.

In *The Hamlet* and *Concarneau*, which he painted between 1909 and 1910, the influence of

A Rib of Beef
1926
Musée
d'Art Moderne
de la ville de Paris

THE SEINE AT CHATOU. 1921
Private Collection, New York

BOATS AT LOW TIDE. 1938
(21" × 25½") Private Collection

Cézanne's style is less noticeable and sometimes hardly apparent; it had obviously begun losing its hold on Vlaminck and in *The Barges* it has disappeared altogether. The new style was already taking shape, and it was to this new style, which for many years made the public forget the two earlier styles, that Vlaminck was to owe his fame.

FROM LONDON TO VALMONDOIS

It was Vlaminck's liking for the banks of the Seine that in 1911 prompted Vollard to suggest that he should go and paint the banks of the Thames. Although Vlaminck had always been curiously reluctant to travel, he set off for London and spent a fortnight there. In his English pictures, *Tower Bridge, Southampton*, etc., his new style is confirmed; in composition and colour it is as far removed from the geometrical structure of the preceding period as it is from the dazzling harmonies of his Fauve period.

Working within the framework of this conception of landscape, which combined an un-

The Port at Martigues. Woodcut (13 ½" × 16½")

Lithograph for an illustration
to Georges Duhamel's book, " Les Hommes abandonnés "

The Glacière Road. Etching (13" × 10") from
" Tableaux de Paris ", published by Editions Emile-Paul, Paris, 1937

deniable force of expression and a fairly mature interpretation of Nature, Vlaminck revealed himself immediately as a master. These pictures, which are painted in wide sweeps of mostly rather dark colour, catch our eye as much by virtue of their rare quality of being able to freeze a moment of time as by their sober passion. For the painter, who was in his full maturity, they certainly represented a perfect compromise between his fiery temperament and his desire to keep it within bounds.

But it seems that Vlaminck was not entirely satisfied with this new way of expressing himself and that he was not fully aware of the personality that his painting was then revealing, or of the importance that it had for his work. For how else are we to explain the fact that for a number of years, during which he painted a whole series of pictures in this new style, the Cézanne manner often reappeared, sometimes quite blatantly as in several views of *Bougival* and *Saint Germain*, and sometimes by implication, as in *The Port at Marseilles*? On the other hand, between 1911 and 1913 he had tried yet another style whose technique was uncertain, and which displayed a certain nonchalance, indeed a limpness that is surprising in a painter endowed with such fertile energy. *The Feather Hat*, *Portrait of Madeleine* and a

Village Street. Pencil drawing

SCENE. Water-colour (17½" × 21"). Private Collection

Self-Portrait painted in 1912 – these leave us perplexed and suggest that Vlaminck was groping indecisively. It is true that he was never much attracted by portrait painting, in spite of the fact that he made some remarkably successful excursions into this field, such as *M. Itasse* (or *Bel Ami*) which has a style all of its own comparable to that of certain of his landscapes such as *The Church at Auvers-sur-Oise*, which he had painted "in homage to Van Gogh" but for once without deriving the usual inspiration from him. But one is led to believe that an artist cannot always recognise what it is that constitutes the true essence of his work, and this has been true of more than one painter.

Throughout the whole of this period, which lasted until about 1927 and whose culminating point can be said have come shortly after he settled in Valmondois (where he had bought a house in 1919 after the great success of his exhibition at Druet's), Vlaminck's work was at a crucial stage where his true personality was most apparent and where, at the same time, his style was a compound of energy and restraint.

I am thinking here of a whole succession of pictures among which we can include *Fishing Port, Suresnes, The Railway Station at Auvers-sur Oise, Burial at Courteilles, The Pontoise Road* and *The Brezolles Road.* In these a sober atmosphere hangs over everything and there is sometimes even a suggestion of torment, but always expressed with great restraint. Even if these pictures were not entirely lacking in poetic sentiment, this sentiment never has the mysterious quality that it has in his late Cézanne pictures, where a tragic gleam appears. Thus in *River Banks,* one of the fine Vlaminck pictures that are preserved in the Musée

The Aqueduct. 1914. Woodcut (10" × 13")

On the Banks of the Oise. Indian ink (16" × 21"). S. Hurwitz Collection, Zurich

d'Art Moderne in Paris, some wispy trees in the foreground stand out in red ochre from a distant village, while still further in the background, a river curves its way under a sky of Prussian blue and black.

And so we see how these various tendencies gradually merged into what was later to be called the Vlaminck style – and this term was used above all to refer to the work he did in this last period. It became possible to speak of Vlaminck's own style because of the consistency, amounting to that of a *leit-motiv*, with which a certain landscape appeared in his work: a road (in the district known as *Ile-de-France* and later as the *Perch*) running across an area of land that the painter has chosen not for its picturesque qualities but rather, it seems, for its nondescript appearance; it looks like so many lumps of earth and as our eyes scan it they linger not so much to admire the spectacle as to draw a life-giving force from it, the same force that impels the march of the seasons, the perpetual round of Nature, the flow of sap in the tree and the ear of corn to swell.

This sense of throbbing life is something we feel in the way Vlaminck painted things, and

LANDSCAPE. 1945. Gouache. Dr. A. Roudinesco Collection, Paris

it even infuses the peasant's cottage, standing between the road and the fields, where we have an apprehension of the toilsome lives of the people that live in it. A landscape by Vlaminck is essentially one of movement. And that is why his roads take us into a realm of sensations and reflections that is quite different from that suggested by Sisley's roads, some of which have the same sort of setting, but along which we are carried into a light-hearted idleness such as we would associate with a Sunday stroller or one musing on idyllic delights, but which is far removed from the quizzical gravity with which the peasant looks at the earth and Vlaminck painted it.

Roads always held a great fascination for him, and they played as important a part in his work as they did in his life. In the difficult days of his youth, he usually made the journey from Paris to Chatou on foot, for lack of the twenty-four sous for the tramfare. Walking on a road through varying scenery is the best way of getting the physical feel of the changing land structures and of discovering their intimate geography. Vlaminck was never to forget these first communings with Nature, his life-long friend.

But the road had also been his livelihood, for he had been a professional racing-cyclist. Then, the pleasure of contemplation had been replaced by the heat of competition and the determination to devour a stretch of road with a pair of wheels. This was only one of the ways in which he sought to satisfy his passion for speed; later on he turned to motorbikes and cars. And here again, more than ever, flashing through the countryside became a violent confrontation, in a great tangle of trees, telegraph-poles and houses, with the road charging triumphantly through the lot.

A "violent confrontation" with landscape glimpsed while travelling at speed – this is precise-

Village Street. Pencil and Indian ink.

ly the impression that was to emerge more and more from Vlaminck's painting. And he often stressed the feeling of movement by overlaying his landscapes with a stormy atmosphere, and as Léon Werth wrote in the preface to the catalogue for the exhibition at the Bernheim-Jeune Gallery in 1920, under " those skies clothed in clouds that have been all creased and crumpled by great kicks in the pants from a Heavenly Father in a polo-neck jersey "

Vlaminck himself has explained (in *The Open Belly*) this curious relation that can exist between the speed at which certain landscapes are seen and the way a feeling of anguish arises and crystallises from them: " An open stretch of country, a man walking along the

FARMHOUSE AND BUILDINGS
Water-colour ($17\frac{1}{2}$" × $23\frac{1}{2}$"). Private Collection

WINTER LANDSCAPE. 1950
Gouache Dr. A. Roudinesco Collection, Paris

road, the face of a town, the walls of a factory, the sombre outline of a forest, suggest, for certain inscrutable reasons, hopes and fears which, in the very speed at which they follow one another, become fused into obscure presentiments that give birth to dreams."

But, in this insight into landscape as seen from the road, and this triumphant progress of one who propels himself, we can also see the equivalent of the act of possession – which tallies very well with what Vlaminck said: " One does not flirt with Nature; one possesses her. One must penetrate her very being."

More and more attracted by the idea of living close to unspoilt Nature, Vlaminck had in 1925 bought La Tourillière, a house out in the country, situated near the village of Rueil-la-Gadalière, in the Eure-et-Loir district. It was then that he added to his work as a painter and writer (he wrote some twenty studies, novels, books of poems and memoirs) the responsibilities of a landowner. And it was here that, thirty years later, he ended his days.

Perhaps it would be going too far if we saw in this retreat into the country a means of satisfying a deep longing for solitude, for that solitude which he called " one of the greatest truths in the world and one of those we fear most ". La Tourillière was not a hermitage and not only did Vlaminck and his wife receive frequent visits from friends, but one or other of the five daughters of his two marriages, Madeleine, Solange, Yolande, Edwige and Godeliève, was always staying with them. Nevertheless, the distance he had put between himself and the capital satisfied his rather imperious demand that he should not be distracted by any city influence from the pursuit of his art – which he was determined should not suffer any changes at the hands of the various movements that in those days were carrying painting into spheres that were quite alien to him. Till the end of his life – that is, till his eighty-second year – Vlaminck painted Vlaminck pictures.

And was he, in this, always true to himself? Yes: in the sense that the pictures he painted at Rueil-la-Gadelière were the true sisters of those he had painted during the preceding period. *The Path in the Snow, The Cottages, Storm at Harvest-time, View from La Tourillière, The Hayricks, The Road from Alençon to Mans* and *The Red Tractor* – these, to mention only a few of the long line of pictures stretching from 1929 to 1956, are stamped unmistakably with Vlaminck's hallmark, as much because of their subjects as the spirit that quickens them. However, there was something new in the way he made a landscape "speak," something connected both with the movement of the brush or knife across the canvas and the thought behind it: not only a greater urgency (echoes of action painting) but also a more explicit realism. To use a rather far-fetched metaphor which is nevertheless apt enough for the lively, bustling tone of his landscapes, we can say that " the reins have been slipped ". Blowing through his painting then was the great wind of lyricism, which seemed to blow up from a dark sky on to everything he looked at: terrified cottages, convulsed trees, bloody suns.

The history of pictorial lyricism has never been written, and in any case it is not certain that it has a history. Isolated cases of it crop up throughout the centuries. When we trace its sources, they seem to merge with those of Romanticism; and in the forms it has taken, it cannot always be distinguished from Baroque. The Renaissance had its lyricism; it consisted in the quasi-theatrical treatment of religious scenes – which in the Middle Ages had always been painted within the narrow limits of mediaeval mysticism and the mediaeval conception of plasticity. And it was through just such a theatrical approach to composition that

STILL-LIFE –
WHISKEY. 1947
(21" × 28½")
Private
Collection
Paris

THE RED TRACTOR. 1956
(15" × 21½") Dr. Sigmond Pollag Collection, Zurich